Trees

Andres Llamas Ruiz

Illustrations by Francisco Arredondo

Sterling Publishing Co., Inc.
New York

Illustrations by Francisco Arredondo
Text by Andres Llamas Ruiz
Translated by Natalia Tizón

Library of Congress Cataloging-in-Publication Data

Llamas Ruiz, Andrés.
   [Árbol. English]
   Trees / Andres Llamas Ruiz.
      p.   cm. — (Cycles of life)
   Includes index.
   Summary: Describes the stages of development in the life of a
trees, from seed to full-grown plant.
   ISBN 0-8069-9327-8
   1. Trees—Juvenile literature.   2. Trees—Life cycles—Juvenile
literature. [1. Trees.] I. Title. II. Series: Llamas Ruiz,
Andrés. Secuencias de la naturaleza. English.
QK475.8.L5813   1996
582.16—dc20   96–25740
                                      CIP
                                      AC

1 3 5 7 9 10 8 6 4 2

Published by Sterling Publishing Company, Inc.
387 Park Avenue South, New York, N.Y. 10016
Originally published in\\\ Spain by Ediciones Estes
©1996 by Ediciones Estes, S.A. ©1996 by Ediciones Lema, S.L.
English version and translation © 1996 by Sterling Publishing Company, Inc.
Distributed in Canada by Sterling Publishing
℅ Canadian Manda Group, One Atlantic Avenue, Suite 105
Toronto, Ontario, Canada M6K 3E7
Distributed in Great Britain and Europe by Cassell PLC
Wellington House, 125 Strand, London WC2R 0BB, England
Distributed in Australia by Capricorn Link (Australia) Pty Ltd.
P.O. Box 6651, Baulkham Hills, Business Centre, NSW 2153, Australia
Printed and Bound in Spain
All rights reserved

Sterling ISBN 0-8069-9327-8

Table of Contents

All trees start their lives as seeds.

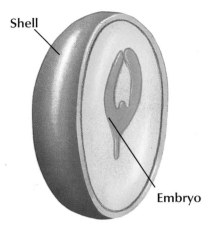

Shell

Embryo

Here you can see the interior of a pinyon tree seed.

For many trees, life starts at the moment a seed reaches the ground. While each tree may produce thousands of seeds, most of them will fall in places that are not suitable for growing, or they may end up being eaten or crushed by animals. So, in fact, only a very small number of seeds survive and become trees.

Trees are living creatures that are born, eat, breathe, grow, reproduce, and die. In order to do all this, trees need certain environmental conditions. This is why a seed will only germinate if it finds enough oxygen and water, if the temperature is adequate, and if it receives the right amount of light, which varies depending on the species.

The future of the seed depends partially on its luck when it reaches the ground. For example, seeds have more difficulty growing in some forests than in others.

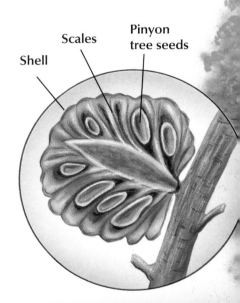

Shell

Scales

Pinyon tree seeds

1. The needles of conifers (evergreens and other cone-bearing trees) take longer to decompose than do the leaves of deciduous trees (those that shed their leaves), and the humus the conifers produce is acidic.

2. This acidity, combined with the fact that conifers prevent a great deal of sunlight from reaching the ground by retaining their needles year-round, makes it hard for new plants to grow in forests dominated by conifers.

3. Plants have more chance to develop in clear patches within the forest.

4. For some types of conifers, the pinecones stay on the branches for some years, while pine nuts fall off gradually.

A large number of seeds end their days being eaten by forest animals, such as squirrels and other rodents. Sometimes, however, seeds are "forgotten" by the animals that have stored them away, allowing the seeds a chance to germinate.

Mushrooms grow well on the ground of a coniferous forest. In the fall, it is surprising to see what a great number of mushrooms there are.

The seed germinates and a small root appears, growing toward the ground.

During the entire winter in temperate areas, the seed waits, asleep. Inside each seed is a reserve of nutrients to keep it alive until the seed has germinated and is ready to start growing. However, not all seeds have the same amount of reserves. Some have only a small supply—just enough to last a few days. Others—such as oak or beech—have enough nutrients to survive the entire winter.

In the spring, the seed wakes up and starts to absorb water. It then swells up and the shell—or seed coat—breaks. At that moment, a tiny root appears, turns toward the ground, and starts to penetrate the ground surface. From the first moment, the root curves downward, in the direction of gravity. Although it is still small, the root itself begins to absorb water and fixes the tree to the ground.

When opening, the seeds of most trees show "fake leaves," called cotyledons. In many instances, these turn green and produce food until the true leaves come out.

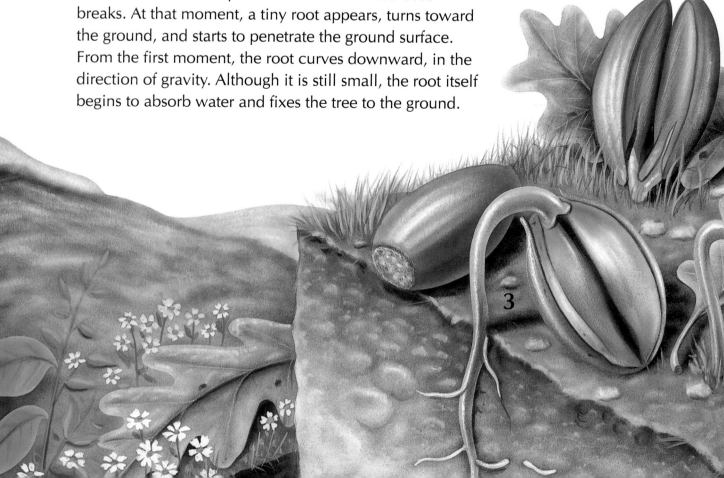

3

Sometimes, seeds have to wait for the right moment to germinate. Here, you can see how an old tree has fallen, creating a clear patch in the forest. This allows enough sunlight for the seeds of new trees to germinate.

The seeds of the white mangrove tree show a very interesting form of adaptation to their swampy habitat. They germinate on the tree and develop a long, pointy taproot that sticks in the mud when the seed falls off the plant. This reduces the risk of being dragged away by the water.

1

2

Germination begins as soon as the days become longer, which is an unmistakable sign that spring is approaching.

1. The embryo grows by living on the seed's reserves of nutrients.

2. The root ends are protected by a resistant cap, which allows the root to penetrate the ground.

3. Oak cotyledons, which are full of nutrients, remain inside the seed shell while a small root comes out and penetrates the ground.

A small stem comes out, growing in search of sunlight.

The first weeks and months of a tree's life are the most critical. The tree is still very small and has not yet developed a defense system to ward off animals and other plants.

During this time, the tree's life is also complex. The root is still small. The tree's real leaves—which, with the roots, will later provide energy for the tree to live and continue growing—have not yet appeared. The first leaves (cotyledons) are not true leaves, since they do not come from buds. The number of these first leaves varies from one to more than a dozen, depending on the tree species. They are very simple leaves with a short life and are usually very different from the leaves of the adult tree.

After the root has penetrated the ground, the seed turns into a seedling that eats the food reserves. The seedling is made up of a tiny root, the cotyledons (which have gradually deteriorated), and a small stem (which starts breaking out to the surface in search of sunlight).

Cotyledons are easy to spot because they usually stick out of the ground, searching for sunlight. They will perform photosynthesis (the process of changing chemicals and light into energy) until the tree starts to develop its real leaves.

1. During the first days of life, beech trees have two flat cotyledons, which help to obtain energy to continue its growth.

2. Fir cotyledons have a very particular shape. Their numbers vary between five and eighteen, depending on the species. They are long and are connected to part of the seed's shell.

3. When the tiny stem starts to come up from the ground, the first real leaves appear.

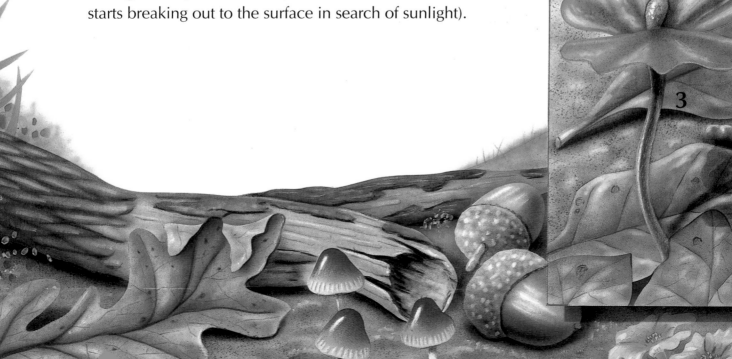

3

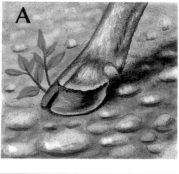

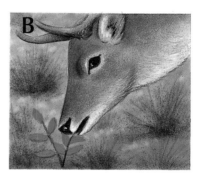

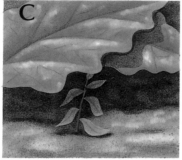

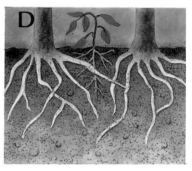

At the beginning, it is difficult to know the precise shape the tree will have when it is fully grown. Here, you can see the features of an Atlas cedar, which lives in the mountains of northern Africa.

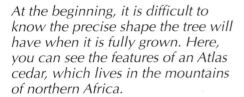

Many dangers threaten the tree during its first days of life. It can be stepped on by animals (A) or eaten (B). The shadows of other, bigger trees may block out the sunlight it needs to grow (C) or the roots of other plants can absorb all the water and nutrients from the ground (D).

9

Later on, the first real leaves unfold from the stem.

When the stem pops out of the ground for the first time, it starts growing upward, searching for sunlight. Gradually, this stem becomes longer. At the end of the stem is a group of cells called the terminal bud, which will later form the new branches and leaves of the tree.

After a certain amount of time (one month for some species), the first real leaves unfold and gradually start to produce food for the tree.

There are also changes underground. The differentiation of cells into specialized root tissues occurs during the first year of the tree's life. From the second year of life onward, the roots become thicker and more resistant, because of the gradual hardening of tubes inside the roots.

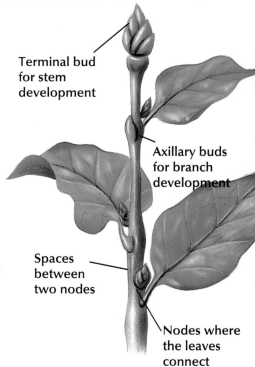

Terminal bud for stem development

Axillary buds for branch development

Spaces between two nodes

Nodes where the leaves connect

Parts of the Stem.

1

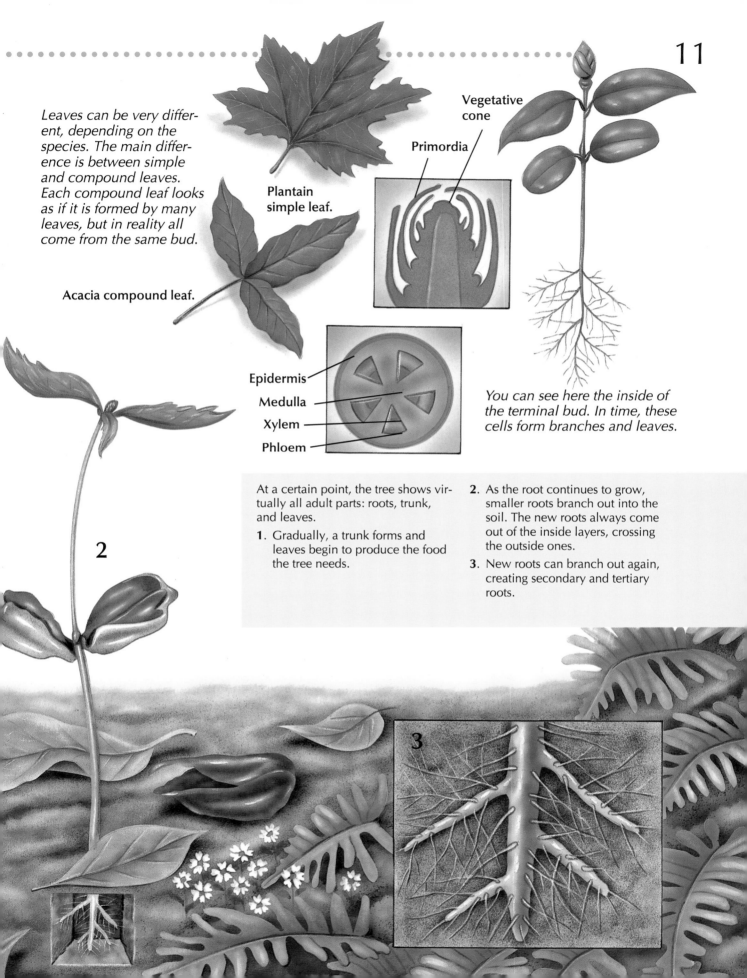

Leaves can be different, depending on the species. The main difference is between simple and compound leaves. Each compound leaf looks as if it is formed by many leaves, but in reality all come from the same bud.

Plantain simple leaf.

Acacia compound leaf.

Primordia

Vegetative cone

Epidermis

Medulla

Xylem

Phloem

You can see here the inside of the terminal bud. In time, these cells form branches and leaves.

2

At a certain point, the tree shows virtually all adult parts: roots, trunk, and leaves.

1. Gradually, a trunk forms and leaves begin to produce the food the tree needs.

2. As the root continues to grow, smaller roots branch out into the soil. The new roots always come out of the inside layers, crossing the outside ones.

3. New roots can branch out again, creating secondary and tertiary roots.

3

The trunk develops bark for protection.

Just below the surface of the trunk, there is a constant flow of substances up and down the tree. Water and mineral salts travel from the roots to the leaves. Nutrients also pass in the other direction, from the leaves to the rest of the tree.

To protect this flow and the trunk in general, the tree forms a skin around itself called the bark, which helps protect the tree from dangers such as animals, fungi, fires, etc. However, the bark is not an indestructible barrier. Many kinds of mushrooms, parasitic plants, and insects are able to penetrate it, stay inside, and "steal" nutrients from the tree. Fungi are especially harmful because they rot the wood and form holes that allow new enemies of the tree to attack.

You can see here tunnels that insects have dug inside a tree trunk. The main one was made by a female beetle who used it to lay her eggs. Others were dug by the larvae after they hatched from the eggs.

The trunk supports the leafy branch systems and transports nutrients between the roots and the leaves. The inside of the branches and the tree trunk are made up of wood. The inner part (the one in the very center) is formed by dry, hard wood that can support the weight of the branches. Surrounding it is live wood, through which the tree's food circulates.

1. The inside layer of the bark is called "cambium" and is formed by millions of live cells that divide. Through them, the sap circulates.

2. While the trunk grows, some cells die and become Xylem (water-conducting tissue) or bark (the tree's outer layer), which forms a defensive barrier against external attacks.

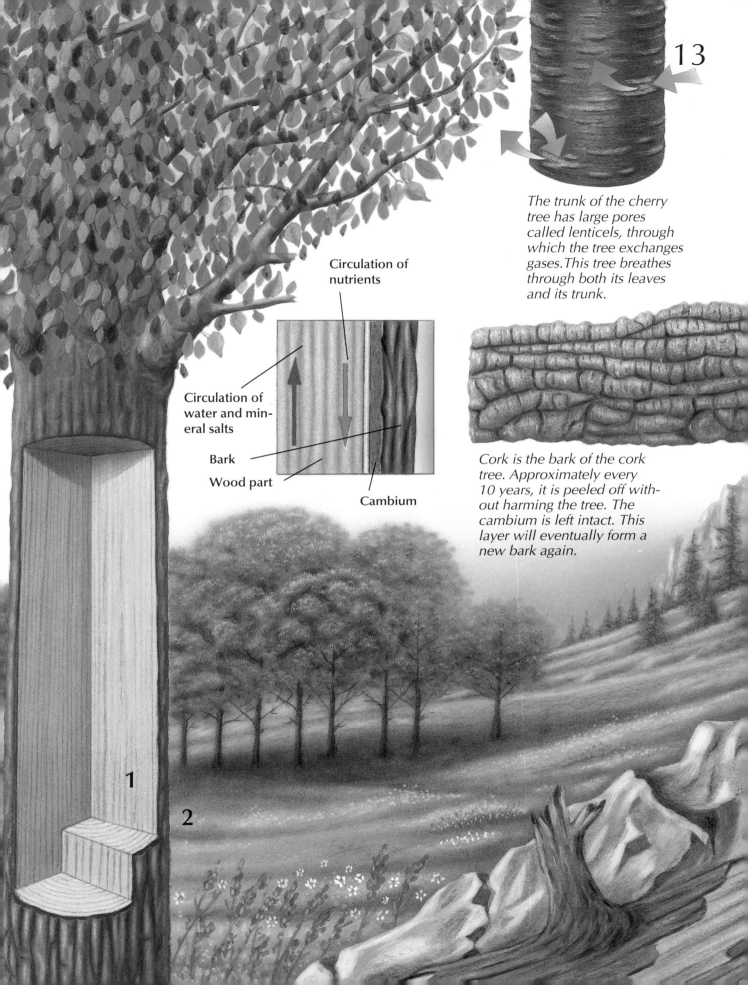

13

The trunk of the cherry tree has large pores called lenticels, through which the tree exchanges gases. This tree breathes through both its leaves and its trunk.

Circulation of nutrients

Circulation of water and mineral salts

Bark

Wood part

Cambium

Cork is the bark of the cork tree. Approximately every 10 years, it is peeled off without harming the tree. The cambium is left intact. This layer will eventually form a new bark again.

1

2

The tree continues to grow in height and in thickness.

Gradually, the stem grows and the branches become longer, always reaching toward the light. The goal is to grow many long branches, which will support a large number of leaves, so that they can produce more food for the tree.

Trees grow in height and thickness. At the end of each branch, a group of cells lengthens the branch as they divide. The tree's diameter also increases. The cambium cells surrounding the woody part of the tree divide sideways, thickening the trunk, branches, and roots. Each year the change in diameter can be up to several inches, depending on the species. Giant sequoias, for example, can increase their diameter by up to 4 inches per year!

Tree branches for each species have specific, characteristic shapes. This is why they can be easily recognized even when some species lose their leaves in the winter. You can see here an oak (A), a fir (B), and a cypress tree (C).

2

1

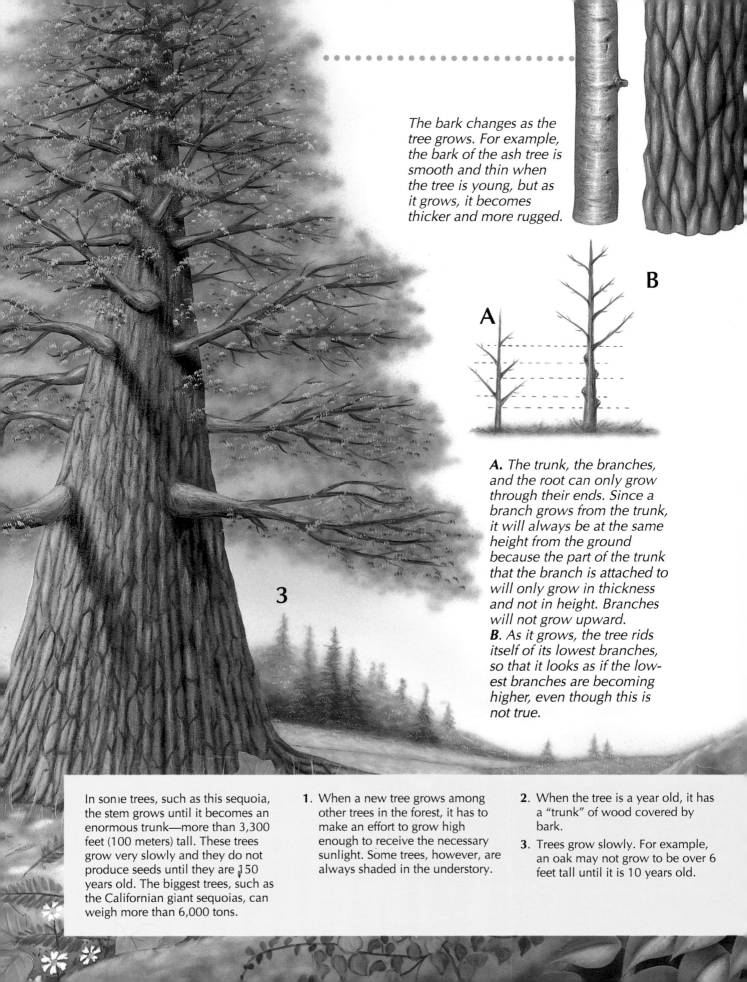

The bark changes as the tree grows. For example, the bark of the ash tree is smooth and thin when the tree is young, but as it grows, it becomes thicker and more rugged.

A

B

A. *The trunk, the branches, and the root can only grow through their ends. Since a branch grows from the trunk, it will always be at the same height from the ground because the part of the trunk that the branch is attached to will only grow in thickness and not in height. Branches will not grow upward.*
B. *As it grows, the tree rids itself of its lowest branches, so that it looks as if the lowest branches are becoming higher, even though this is not true.*

3

In some trees, such as this sequoia, the stem grows until it becomes an enormous trunk—more than 3,300 feet (100 meters) tall. These trees grow very slowly and they do not produce seeds until they are 150 years old. The biggest trees, such as the Californian giant sequoias, can weigh more than 6,000 tons.

1. When a new tree grows among other trees in the forest, it has to make an effort to grow high enough to receive the necessary sunlight. Some trees, however, are always shaded in the understory.

2. When the tree is a year old, it has a "trunk" of wood covered by bark.

3. Trees grow slowly. For example, an oak may not grow to be over 6 feet tall until it is 10 years old.

The roots provide water and mineral salts to the tree.

The millions of little hairs covering the surface of the roots absorb water and mineral salts for the plant. First, the water travels to the smaller roots, then to the main roots, and finally to the trunk and leaves.

When the spring comes, the roots are the first part of the tree to become active. Only the youngest part of the root, which is located close to the root end and covered with tiny hairs, can actually absorb water and mineral salts. Each one of the root hairs is equal to a single cell and will live a maximum of a couple of months. When the fall comes, all the root hairs die.

The roots spread out and cover a large area in order to absorb enough water. Some species sink their roots deep into the ground to reach the water they need. Other trees, which grow where water is close to the surface, have very shallow roots. In this case, the root system spreads horizontally to cover large areas (sometimes even larger than a soccer field), but penetrate only a couple of feet into the ground.

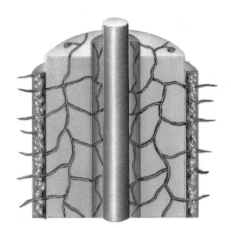

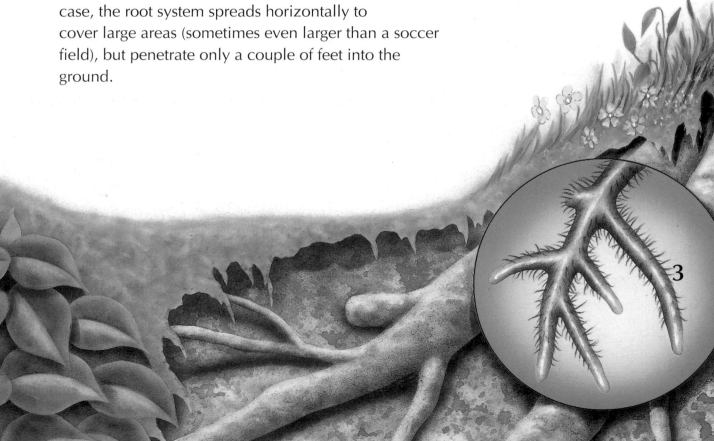

3

The roots of trees, such as pines and oaks, have a symbiotic relationship with mushrooms. The mushrooms produce substances that favor absorption by the root hairs. In exchange, they receive nutrients from the root. What a partnership!

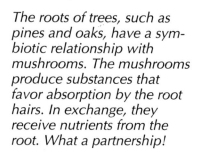

Mangrove trees grow in flooded coastal areas. In order to do this, they have two kinds of roots: respiratory roots (which appear above the water, during the low tide, to get oxygen) and support roots (which form arches and fix themselves in the mud).

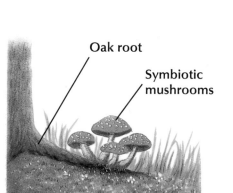

Oak root

Symbiotic mushrooms

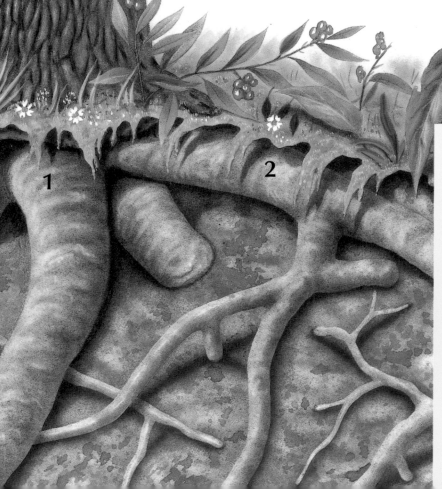

1

2

As the tree grows, it needs more food, which explains why its roots must continue to grow. Apart from supporting the tree, the roots absorb ground water, which is full of the mineral salts the tree needs to produce food. The water travels from the roots to the leaves.

1. The main root sinks downward. It has the shape of an axis.

2. The secondary roots grow around the main root, securing the tree so that it does not fall. The youngest roots collect water and nutrients. The oldest ones are more woody and support the tree.

3. At the tip of every root is a protective layer of cells called the calyptra.

Deciduous trees are prepared to spend the winter resting without leaves.

At the end of the first summer of life, the young tree must prepare to face the hard winter as if it were an adult. You already know that during the first year the tree is fragile and must defend itself from many enemies. It could even die from the cold during the first winter. This is the hardest stage in a tree's life; if it survives these first months, it will have a good chance to live a long life.

Throughout the year, trees go through changes, depending on the seasons. During the summer, the tree works tirelessly, while in the winter it lives at a very slow pace, waiting for the arrival of spring. Winter conditions are not appropriate for the growth of the tree; it is cold and there is very little light. That is why the tree "rests" during this season. When sunlight hours begin to decrease, the tree starts to produce and store reserves. This storage process is finished at the beginning of the fall, and the leaves gradually stop working. Then they lose their green color and turn yellow, orange, or red as they dry.

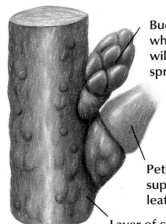

Bud from which the leaf will grow next spring

Petiole, which supports the leaf

Layer of cells

When the fall comes, a barrier is formed at the base of the leaf which will slowly cause the leaf to die. However, this barrier will close the "wound" that will be left after the leaf has fallen off the branch.

Because of food sent by the leaves, the tree can produce a new layer of "new wood" just underneath the bark. This is its way of "gaining weight," or growing in diameter. Every year, the tree and its branches form a new ring of wood.

1

Both deciduous and evergreen trees lose their leaves. The difference is that deciduous trees lose them all at once during the fall, whereas evergreens always keep some of their green leaves.

In temperate climates, growth in both height and width happens only in the spring and summer. The cambium grows toward the outside, and the new cells that appear form very visible rings. Each ring is equal to one stage in growth, which is one year.

1. The leaves that fall on the ground in the fall make the humus layer or leaf litter.

2. When they are covered by other leaves, they are broken down by bacteria and fungi that live among the dead leaves.

3. Then the leaf decomposes and turns into humus, which feeds new plants and helps them to grow.

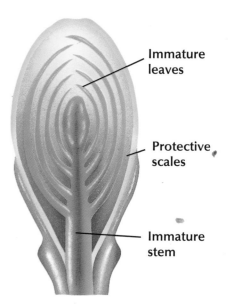

Immature leaves

Protective scales

Immature stem

Spring covers the tree with leaves.

When the spring comes and sunlight hours increase, the tree starts to awaken. It has spent the winter with bare, leafless branches, but its sprouts have been protected inside thick buds, waiting for spring. The buds contain the substances that the tree needs to grow quickly when good weather arrives. The sprouts will swell and the leaves and flowers will come out. The new leaves will soon begin to produce food for the tree by absorbing sunlight energy.

In order to absorb light, the leaves need chlorophyll—a green pigment that gives the leaves their color. When the leaves have little chlorophyll, they turn yellowish in color, as they do in the fall. During the summer, however, the leaves grow. Each tree can have hundreds of thousands of leaves on its branches, and all of them have only one goal: to feed the tree. In order to get the greatest amount of sunlight possible, leaves grow on trees without casting shadows on one another.

Inside the buds are all the necessary parts for growth. The bud is a very delicate organ. Its cells have very thin walls. In order to protect them during the winter, the tree covers them with special leaf-like or scale-like structures called bud scales.

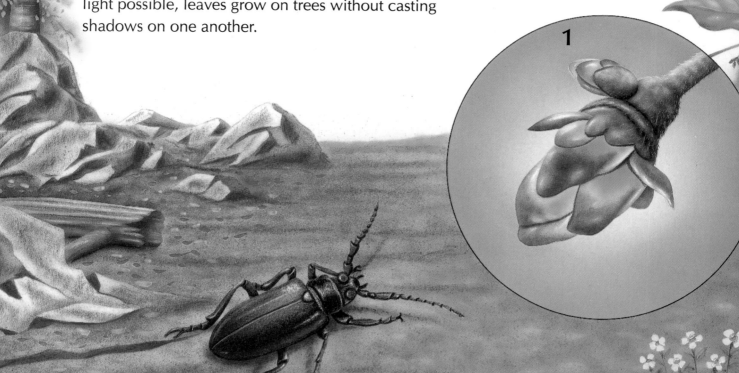

1

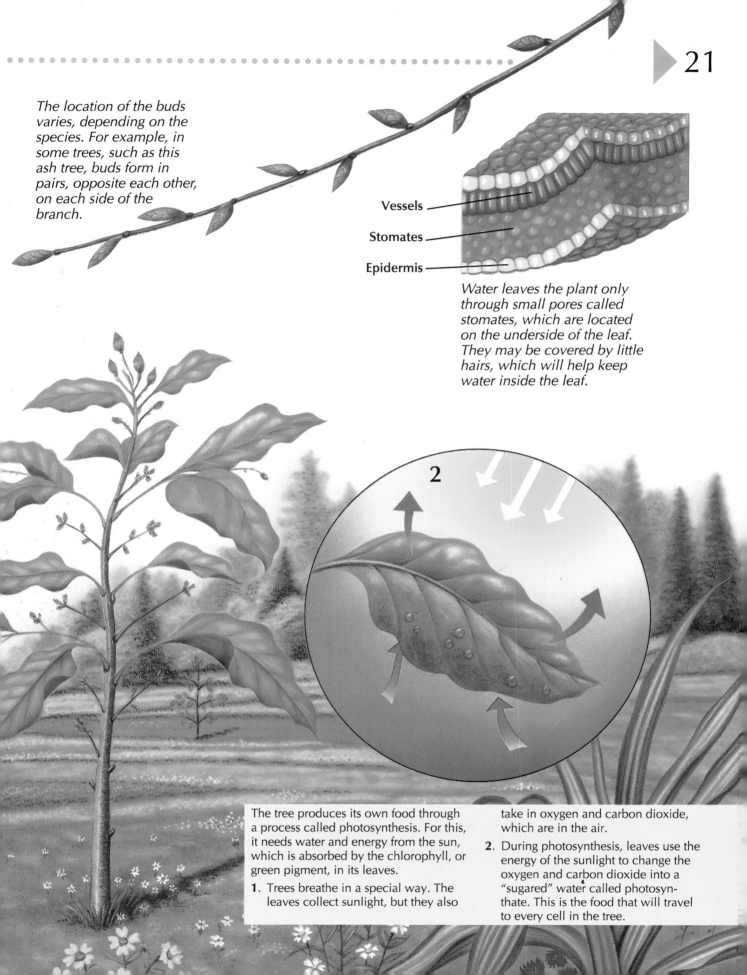

The location of the buds varies, depending on the species. For example, in some trees, such as this ash tree, buds form in pairs, opposite each other, on each side of the branch.

Vessels

Stomates

Epidermis

Water leaves the plant only through small pores called stomates, which are located on the underside of the leaf. They may be covered by little hairs, which will help keep water inside the leaf.

2

The tree produces its own food through a process called photosynthesis. For this, it needs water and energy from the sun, which is absorbed by the chlorophyll, or green pigment, in its leaves.

1. Trees breathe in a special way. The leaves collect sunlight, but they also take in oxygen and carbon dioxide, which are in the air.

2. During photosynthesis, leaves use the energy of the sunlight to change the oxygen and carbon dioxide into a "sugared" water called photosynthate. This is the food that will travel to every cell in the tree.

In spring, the flowers bloom, adding color to the trees in the forest.

When the spring comes, many trees are filled with flowers that bloom from the sprouts the tree grew the year before. After they have been pollinated, these flowers will turn into fruits, which will produce seeds.

In some cases, flowers combine both male and female parts. In others, separate male and female flowers will grow on the same tree. In still other cases, the sexes grow on separate trees—male on one, female on another. Flowers can vary enormously in both shape and size, ranging from very small to enormous. Flowering systems of some palm trees can grow to be over 300 feet tall, whereas some other trees have flowers that will only grow to a few inches high. The flowers can grow separately, but most often they grow together in systems or clusters.

Some trees have separate "sexes," in which male and female flowers grow on different trees. In this case, we say that the tree is dioecious.

1

The flower is the reproductive organ of the tree. When it is fully developed, the anthers of the stamens open and the pollen grains are released. This process is called dehiscence of the anther.

1. Some flowering trees and some conifers are anemophilous, which means they are pollinated by the wind. To make this process simpler, the flowers grow at the very end of the branches.

2. When the wind blows, millions of pollen grains fall and form yellowish "clouds."

Catkin of a
willow tree.

In many trees, the
male flowers form
long catkins, which
produce thousands—
even millions—of
pollen grains.

Catkin of a
hazelnut tree.

Did you know that some
fruit trees start to bloom
before the leaves come out?
As you can see, inside each
bud a group of compact
flowers forms before the new
leaves appear.

2

The tree pollinates the flowers with the help of the wind or insects.

Male flowers of the "anemophilous" trees release clouds of yellowish powder, or pollen, which travels in the wind. The goal is to reach a female flower of the same species. Pollen weighs so little that it can be carried huge distances by the wind. However, the system is not very precise, which means that great amounts of pollen must be produced. It is thought that out of every million grains of pollen, only one achieves its objective.

There are also entomophilous trees, which are pollinated by insects. The flowers of these trees are much more flashy than the ones in the anemophilous trees and they usually contain nectar, which is rich in sugar. The flowers attract insects, which help to pollinate the trees. The pollen grains of these flowers are much bigger, and are covered by hooks and substances that help them stick to the body of the insect as it travels from one tree to another, transporting pollen from flower to flower and tree to tree.

Wind transports the yellowish clouds formed by millions of tiny grains of pollen.

2

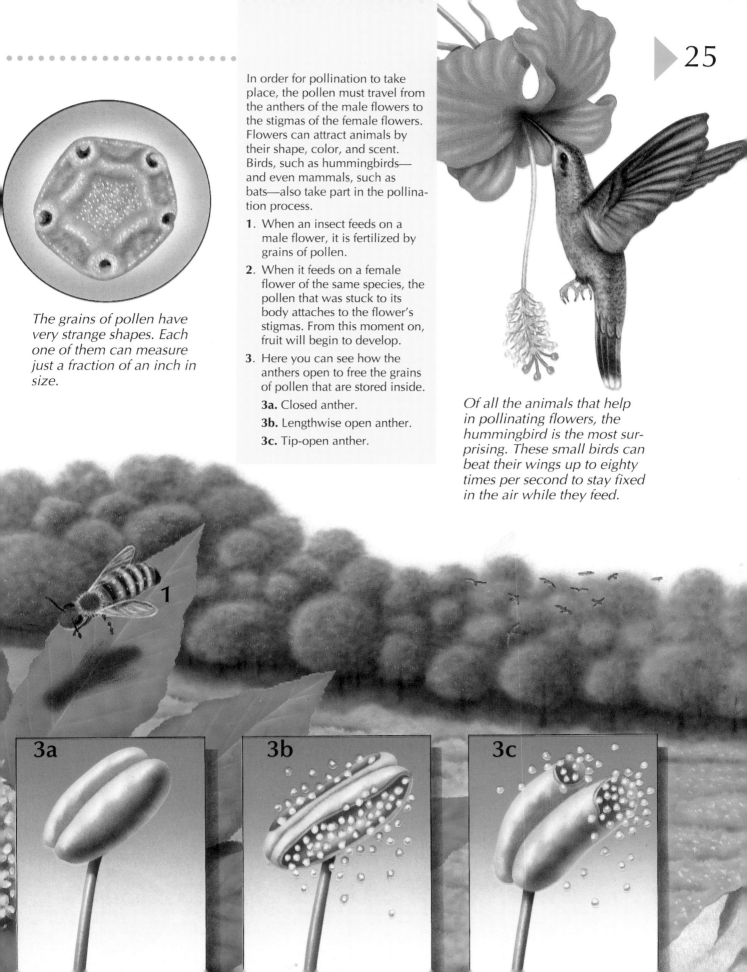

The grains of pollen have very strange shapes. Each one of them can measure just a fraction of an inch in size.

In order for pollination to take place, the pollen must travel from the anthers of the male flowers to the stigmas of the female flowers. Flowers can attract animals by their shape, color, and scent. Birds, such as hummingbirds—and even mammals, such as bats—also take part in the pollination process.

1. When an insect feeds on a male flower, it is fertilized by grains of pollen.

2. When it feeds on a female flower of the same species, the pollen that was stuck to its body attaches to the flower's stigmas. From this moment on, fruit will begin to develop.

3. Here you can see how the anthers open to free the grains of pollen that are stored inside.

   3a. Closed anther.

   3b. Lengthwise open anther.

   3c. Tip-open anther.

Of all the animals that help in pollinating flowers, the hummingbird is the most surprising. These small birds can beat their wings up to eighty times per second to stay fixed in the air while they feed.

3a

3b

3c

Once pollinated, flowers become fruit.

When pollen reaches the flower's stigma, it absorbs some liquid and swells. It then forms the pollen tube, which is an extension that enters the style to reach the ovary. Once there, it comes into contact with the ovule, and as a result the male and female cells unite. This is how fertilization occurs.

After fertilization, there are big changes in the flower. The biggest ones occur in the ovary, whose walls grow and can lead to two kinds of results:

In the first case, the ovary walls build up woody tissue to protect the seed tip. In this case, dried fruit, such as hazelnuts, walnuts, and almonds are formed.

In the second case, the walls of the ovary develop pulpy tissue and produce fleshy fruit such as peaches and cherries.

As you can see, trees can product very different kinds of fruit:
A. Hawthorne pomes
B. Plums
C. Oranges
D. Lemons
E. Pineapples
F. Oak acorns

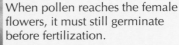

1

When pollen reaches the female flowers, it must still germinate before fertilization.

1. The grain of pollen has reached the stigma of the female flower.

2. The pollen tube begins to form. It enters the ovary.

3. When the tube reaches the ovary, the sexual cells of the male and female flower unite. This is fertilization.

Berries are very important in the diet of many forest animals.

Coconuts can travel long distances, floating on the sea before arriving at another coast. Once there, the coconut "milk" allows the seed to grow in the dry sand of the beach.

Mature pollen

Stigma

Style

Ovary

2

3

Ovules (female sexual cells)

Pollen tube

Male sexual cells

The seeds inside the fruit will look for a place to grow.

In trying to distribute their seeds, trees have the same trouble as in pollination. If a seed falls under the tree it came from, it usually will not be able to grow. That is why the seed needs to travel far away until it finds the best conditions for germination and growth.

The fruit's casings influence the way the seeds are distributed. There are three main systems: air, water, and animals. In the first case, some fruits or seeds have "winged" outgrowths, which allow them to travel with the wind. On the other hand, the seeds of many trees that live along riverbanks travel by water; their casings have air-containing tissues or watertight chambers that keep them floating downstream until they reach the banks where they will grow.

The trees you probably know best are the ones that produce colorful, tasty fruit, which attracts animals and birds. In this case, the animal eats the fruit and unknowingly contributes to spreading the seeds.

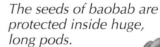

The seeds of baobab are protected inside huge, long pods.

The intervention of animals is important in spreading the seeds of many trees. In this "pact," the animal obtains food and the tree's seeds travel a longer distance than if they had simply fallen off.

1. Birds nibble on the tasty fruit.

2. When the bird flies, some seeds fall with its excrement; in this way, the bird helps distribute fruit seeds as it flies through the forest.

3. Some trees have well protected seeds (remember the hard nutshell) that can only be opened by certain animals, such as squirrels.

4. Squirrels conserve their food supplies to prepare for the hard winter. That is why they bury large amounts of seeds and nuts in many parts of their territory.

5. During the winter, they dig up and eat the food they have hidden. Sometimes they are unable to dig up all the seeds from their hiding places and the seeds remain, well protected underground, until the arrival of spring.

These seeds have curious "membrane-like wings." As they fall to the ground, they spiral down like helicopters.

Not all fruit is easy for animals to eat. Here, you can see the thorny shell that protects the seed of a chestnut tree. Inside are the tasty chestnuts.

Despite the cyclical sequence of its life, no tree lives forever...

The tree is not usually alone but lives in a forest, surrounded by other trees with which it must compete. If the tree lives alone, it may grow stronger because it receives more sunlight. As a result, it may live longer.

During its entire life, the tree has to fight with its surroundings. It must compete with other trees for light and nutrients, defend itself from attacks of parasitic plants, and protect itself from being devoured by plant-eating animals—from tiny insects to big mammals. Some animals pierce the trunk to build their nests; others eat the leaves and bark. Therefore, when the tree cannot find all that it needs, it can develop very poorly or even stop growing. In this case, the tree normally changes its lifestyle to adapt to the hard conditions, but sometimes it can become sick or even die. It is not always easy being a tree.

When they get to a certain age, trees stop growing in height, but continue to increase in diameter because food is always circulating inside the ring of new wood that is grown every year. Here, you can see a bristlecone pine, which is native to the Rocky Mountains. It grows slowly, but it can live more than 4,600 years!

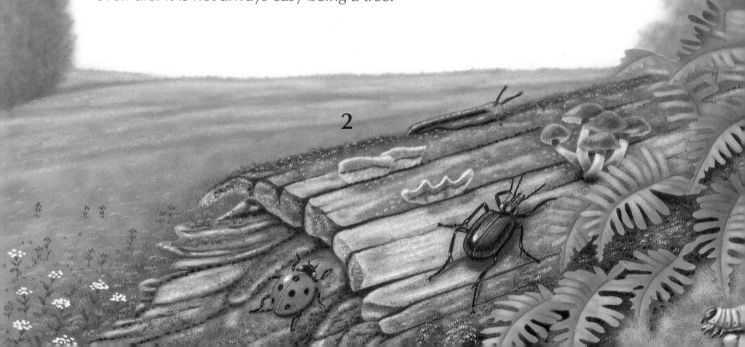

2

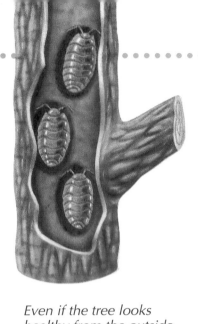

Even if the tree looks healthy from the outside, inside it may be suffering from attacks of insect larvae or fungi.

A holm oak can be attacked by many different insects. As you can see, they use practically all parts of the tree to lay their eggs.

Some trees form galls, which are tumor-like growths that are produced in response to an infection or an attack by an insect or fungus. Some insects, such as parasitic wasps, use galls as a place for their larvae to grow safely.

Finally, there is a moment when the tree cannot keep on fighting, and it dies.

1. Disease, lightning, and fires may also cause its death. However, the dead tree continues to give life by becoming a perfect place for other vegetation—such as mushrooms, ferns and moss—to grow in.

2. The fallen trunk of the dead tree is soon occupied by a large number of plants and animals that use it for food, shelter, and growth support.

3. However, there are already some seeds in the forest ground, waiting to grow and form a new generation of trees.

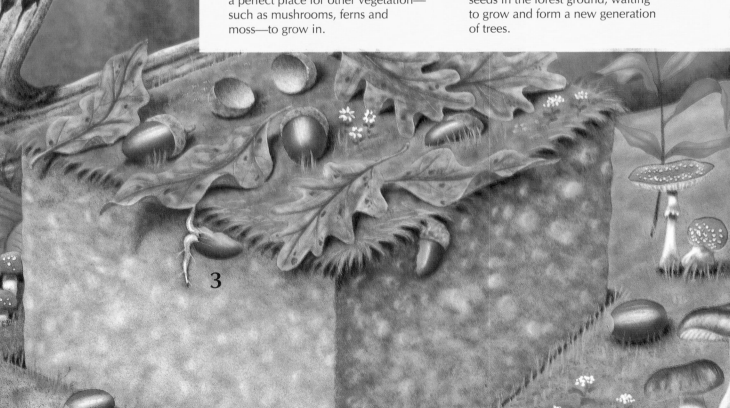

Glossary

Gall-nuts: Protrusions formed on some trees that are caused by insects making tiny holes to deposit their eggs.

Anemophilous: Plant that is pollinated by the wind.

Deciduous: Plant that sheds its leaves annually.

Stigma: A widened, sticky part of the style that is intended to receive the grains of pollen from the stamens.

Fertilization: The moment at which a male sex cell penetrates an ovule (female sex cell), thus beginning the development of a new plant.

Photosynthesis: The process by which green plants combine organic matter from carbon dioxide by using light as a source of energy.

Germinate: To sprout or put forth roots from the seed.

Inflorescence: The manner in which flowers arrange themselves on a given stem or branch.

Lignification: The process by which certain parts of the plant become woody because of an increase in the concentration of lignin.

Nectar: A substance rich in sugar that is secreted by the flowers of certain plants in order to attract the insects they need for pollination.

Ovule: The female reproductive cell that is produced within the ovary of the plant.

Evergreen: Plant that keeps its leaves year-round (opposite of deciduous).

Pigments: Organic substances responsible for giving a plant colors.

Pollination: The displacement or passing of pollen from the anthers (male reproductive organs) to the stigmas (female reproductive organs).

Seed: Ripe fertilized ovule which will generate an adult plant.

Symbiosis: Cohabitation of two living beings to mutual advantage. Sometimes the relationship is so intimate that one cannot live without the other.

Buds: Shoots that form in the axil of leaves or at the end of a stem or branch. They contribute to the growth of the plant.

Index